Castleberry Cove
Poems for the Journey

By: Lori Williams

Planet Castleberry Press

Copyright © 2022 Planet Castleberry Press

All Rights Reserved

"No part of this publication may be reproduced, distributed, or transmitted in any form or by any means, including photocopying, recording, or other electronic or mechanical methods, or by any information storage and retrieval system without the prior written permission of the publisher, except in the case of very brief quotations embodied in critical reviews and certain other noncommercial uses permitted by copyright law."

Table of Contents

Part 1:

Emotion

7

Part 2:

Enough

21

Part 3:

Energy

32

Part 4:

Escape

45

Part 5:

Excitement

59

Part 6:

Eternity

69

Introduction

Welcome to Castleberry Cove.

This is a place where dreams are made, and future memories come true. This is my place where intuition, insight, and information are downloaded and I can create. I hope you too, can find relaxation, escape, and imagination at Castleberry Cove.

You are about to embark on a journey told through poems. They will capture your thoughts and attention in a way that perhaps you didn't even know was there waiting to be expressed.

Each of us goes through our own passageways in life and they lead us to new discoveries about ourselves in a way that is very personal to each of us.

My hope is that everyone that takes in these words in my poems finds their own place of retreat, renewal, and personal escape.

You too can go into your own Castleberry Cove, where you are able to dream and be free.

Free from the restraints of society, the mind, and any other restrictions you or someone else may have placed on you.

At the end of each chapter, you will have space to journal your own thoughts & insights about that particular topic.

You were meant for more. You were meant to awaken to your soul's purpose and destiny. May Castleberry Cove take you there...

Part 1:

Emotion

We feel emotion daily. It can come in a range of levels from the deepest depths of sadness and overwhelm to elation and bliss. It's how we express these emotions is what often gets us to the next phase. Do we allow them to overcome us and take us out of the game? Or do we allow them to process through and get us to where we need to be?

Getting out of our minds, which are largely focused on the ego part of our brains, is half the battle. When we look for our true feelings, they are rooted in intuition which is often surprising, exciting, and maybe even catches you off guard a bit. *When you feel that, you know you are in an authentic and true emotional state.*

This first segment of poems will reflect on the various levels of emotions that we feel. Those emotions will be expressed through imagery and feelings that will help propel you to look at your own and thereby not become so attached to them. But rather view them as a cloud floating by that you can observe and learn from at the same time.

So, let's escape to Castleberry Cove and explore our emotions through poetry.

Purging Your Shadows

The final cleanout

The final purge of the layers so deep

The ones that have kept you trapped

And the ones you want to keep

They feel familiar, frustrating, yet somehow safe

That's just the illusion of the mind to keep you from your fate

The final exit, the final time

That you must face this karmic rhyme

The one that reinvents itself

The one that shows you your true self

The last trip around the moon is here

To show you where you have room

To grow, to clean, to glean, to clear

To unlock the things that keep you from moving forward

But that's just an illusion, in order to heal, you must move toward

The things that scare you and paralyze you from upward growth

They are your teachers, your healers, and your unspoken hope

Middle of the Green

So many emotions running through like a locomotion

All the feels, they all feel so real

Trapped in the mind, that is where you find, the confusion

They are not the real emotion, only an illusion

Rest in your heart center, remove the processing, & disparity

That is where you will get the clarity

Signs and symbols are helpful

But not when you try to decipher with fear & are doubtful

Remove the logic, remove the analyzing

Stop in the middle of the green

And all will soon be revealed and seen

Trying to get insight when you are locked in the past or future

Removes your ability to see the now, the present

And all you hope for

All the feels, they all feel so real

Let the tears flow if need be

But check yourself first, if that is the reality

The universe won't communicate in fear, strife, or conflict

It's gentle, soft, surprising, and often quick

Stay in the now, rest in your heart center

For that is the place of revelation without hinder

Unaware Dance

Lighted butterfly on the wings of the night

So dazzling in the dance of the flight

Electric clouds that rage with the EDM beat

You can feel from head to heart to hands and feet

The echo of the bass, the rhythmic drum of step and time

All penetrate the emotions of anticipatory signs

So close, so near

Like the buzz of a bumble bee flying past the ear

Breaking it down to the high vibratory beat

You feel so alive, so you, so totally free

Thoughts turn to emotions and emotions turn to expression

Let it all flow in your beautiful contractions and compressions

Don't hold back, let it all out

Just be you and live in your now

Soon

Dreaming of redemption, dreaming of release
Ready for a new heaven, new earth, & new beliefs
Dropping the fear so it no longer controls
Distancing myself from all the strongholds

Trusting for more, trusting for peace
Relaxing, waiting, breathing, restoring through relief
"Hold on, not much longer", the gentle angel whispers
"Hold on, look up, I'm here, no more fears"

We all feel it, it's not just you
You're not alone, we all want it too
Together we will win, together we will fly
High, high above, into the rainbow-filled sky

Breathe. Breathe. Breathe.
The time is so close at hand
You're doing the work and will soon hear the command
To fly to the sky with hope, peace, and love
That's it, we're now going, high up above

Soul Mates

I'm here now, I'll help wipe the tears

I'm here now, I'll listen to your fears

You are mine; I am yours

Together we'll face over 1000 years

You never have to be alone

You never will cry alone

For we found each other and together we form

A perfect bond, a perfect circle, that can never be torn

A bond only you and I keep

For it's been ours through lifetimes with a love oh so sweet

We'll never give up, we'll never back down

For we are 2 hearts intertwined with the cosmic love sound

It's gentle, it's sweet, it's always near

It knows the innermost thoughts of hope, love, peace, & fear

Rest on my shoulder, rest in my arms

Wherever you feel safest from the alarms

I'm not leaving, I'll fight for you to the end

You are my love, my heart, and my best friend

Learning Lessons

Trying to make the best decision

But with limited information

Don't try to work it out now

You'll have the answer in due time

It will all be clear, do not fear

Stay in integrity, we will lead you to safety

Don't worry, don't process, sit and be

We won't steer you wrong, you are amazing

You did nothing wrong, you spoke your truth

That's all we wanted just for you

You are learning the boundaries

You are learning the patterns

That's all this was

A lesson in the return of Saturn

You won't make a bad choice

We will make it clear

You have nothing to lose, the end of all of this is coming near

Hang on dear one, you've completed your mission

For the next step is coming, all you've been hoping for and wishing

Let It Go

Get out of your head, get out of your head

Listen, listen, listen to what we've said

Rest in the knowing that we've got you

You need to relax, we always tell the truth

We won't let you fall; we won't let you go

You are so much more powerful than you even know

Listen to us, please let it go, we will give you peace & hope

Don't worry about the present situations

They will all fade away soon like a constellation

Let it go, dear friend, we won't let you fall

Lift your head, stand up tall

You know what matters; you know what's best

Listen to us and forget the rest

We're here, we got you

We know what, where, how, and who

Those issues weighing so heavy on the mind

Are nothing to fear, for they aren't worth the time

Let it go, let it go, enjoy your life

You'll love what's coming

It will put an end to this strife in your life

Let It Come

Let it come, let it play out

You don't have to force, you don't have to shout

No need to control, no need to get emotional

Let it come, let it all come in time

You will be surprised, by the light in your eyes

When you see the magic arrive

Knowing you didn't have to manipulate

But simply just articulate

What you wanted, what you needed, what you all planned out

The rhythm of the flow is about to unfold

You don't have to second guess

It's all coming as it should

And not by happenstance

Let it come, let it flow

Let the mysteries of the universe unfold

It's a gift waiting to be unwrapped

It's coming. don't start too early, it won't be too late

We never hesitate

The perfect time, the perfect rhyme

To wrap up this chapter in which you find

All will come to fruition- just shhh, listen, listen, listen

Tethered Hearts

The life partner you chose, you chose before the now

You've always been connected, electric, and yet somehow

You are still you; they are still them

But in a calculated dance, you find your rhythms

The joy of being alive, on the inside

Is what you bring together

No matter the journey, the path

You two will always weather

The highs, the lows, the then, the now

The shifts in consciousness all make sense of everything somehow

No need to control, no need to argue

Embrace the differences and they will find them; you will find you

Some call it soul mates or a twin flame

No matter the name, it's all the same

They may look familiar, like a memory from the future or past

Look into their eyes, it's true love at last

You were always meant to do this journey together

From before time, your hearts were and are, eternally tethered

You Be You

Unique, diverse, creative, expressive
You Be You
Don't let anyone squelch that or be dismissive

Captivating, deep, engaging, and fun
You Be You
The cosmic personality of depth has just begun

You Be You
Shining and True
True to You
You Be You

You Be You
Honest and True
True to You
You Be You

Confident, compassionate, dedicated, calculated
You Be You
With all the universal force to be articulated

Surprising, energizing, charming, and authentic
You Be You
Be what you are, the unstoppable eccentric

You Be You
Light and True
True to You
You Be You

Delayed Response

Pushing internally to find the answer inside of me

Seeking, wanting, waiting, fusing

I know it's coming; I know it's rushing

Rushing straight to me from up above

I've already planned it out of my own love

It feels delayed but it's right on course, it's right on time

It feels withheld but it's actually there to find

I try to hold my breath with an anxious refrain

For I know the frenetic energy only delays the game

Ready to go to the next level and complete this course

So many lessons to learn, yet there's still a restless force

Shh, calm down, breathe my love

The answers are coming within you delivered from up above

A delayed response is just a whisper because

It came from the universe telling you to go within and pause

Part 1: Emotion
Thoughts & Insights

What emotions do you need to express?

Part 2:

Enough

Ever felt like you were just at the end of your rope? Whether it be personally, professionally, or even your global perspective. We all get there; we all feel that frustration when we believe we'd had enough.

It's a natural part of the human experience. It's the constant paradox of push and pull to get to that balance where all feels right within us.

Without the feelings of exasperation, we would stay stagnant and complacent. Oftentimes humans want to rush through this stage because they think if they aren't happy and have "high vibes" then something is wrong with them. But it's entirely the opposite.

To get through this chapter of our lives we must feel that resistance in ourselves and allow it to push us through to our greatness.

This part of our journey allows us to express that stage of our lives where we need to feel something to get where we want to be. Highs and lows are all part of the process as we push ahead to that moment of awakening to who we truly are. Just like the balance of light and dark, we allow ourselves to shine that light into those corners and bring forth the rainbow inside.

Life Isn't Just Happening to Us

The biggest turn of events, the biggest flip

Life isn't just happening to us, no, this isn't a trick

When you wake up and realize

That all is happening right before your eyes

Is actually created for you, by you

I know it sounds crazy, but it's all true

You aren't just in this job, this school, this relationship

You picked it all out, created it, and made it all fit

Into the life you wanted, to learn the lesson

To figure out the next level, and find your passion

Seeing yourself in the same loop after loop

Meeting the same kinds of people

Making you jump through the same hoop after hoop

It's not a coincidence, it's not a judgment

No, it's to help you level up for ascension

To raise to the highest you can possibly be

To be yourself, break out of the program, and be fully free

Drained

The draining sinking of the soul feeling

When you are not doing what you should be doing

You know it well

The one where your heart & your expenses

Are on opposite sides of the scale

The longing to be in your career and passion of choice

Only to wake up and realize you're stuck, and can't find your voice

It's a draining of the resources that you came in with

You know there is more to life than just this

A life of creativity is breaking down the door

And saying, what more are you waiting for?

Surrender to the fears, take the leap of faith

What could be worse than a life lived in waste?

The soul-sucking life only lived for the paper-pushing matrix

Is no life at all and eventually your creativity will cease to exist

You can't live in a drained pained restless state

Your time is here and now

Don't make the day just "good", make it great

Cashing In on Life's Directions

Between the avenue of confusion and lost

Is the sign that says "this isn't the life you bought"

There are no refunds, only do-overs, and re-crafters

But why do that when you can complete it all in this chapter?

Look for the path that lights up and brings you joy

This is the direction you belong

You know which one, don't act so coy

Left, right, up, down, it can feel like a lot

If you don't know where to be found and how to be sought

Your purpose and passion are calling

They aren't far from you, you are not falling

You only need to look up

Press the accelerator & fill your own cup

The roadway through life is winding and challenging

But don't stay at the stoplight paralyzed and following

The crowds and masses who only live for the surfaces

That's right, there so much more than what you think it is

You were meant for more than average

You were meant for excitement, even among the challenges

No buyer's remorse here, you came in with more than despair & fear

So start living that abundant life of greatness

It's on the corner of Fifth Dimension Street & Awareness

Cut the Cord

Cut the cord to the things weighing you down

Cut the tethered rod that's holding you to the ground

Anything that no longer serves you needs to be released

You don't have to be restricted to the past, it's time for sweet relief

Cut the cord of attachment, false hopes, victim mindsets, & illusions

Awaken to a new coil, one that goes directly up to the heavens

Those old entrapments, entangled with people

That is no longer meant for you

It's time to step into the now that was created in harmony and truth

Cut the cord of worldly traps that only serve one thing

To strip away your power, and set you up for suffering

That's not what you came for

You deserve abundance, you deserve more

You were designed for this

Harken back your birthright and stop playing defense

Control

Holding on like a vice grip

Holding on so that it won't slip

Anger, rage, fury, all brimming to the top

Oh, why do they ignore me, when will it all stop?

Gotta control, gotta manipulate, gotta persuade, gotta rage

It festers, it boils, it seethes, it coils

So angry you gotta share then overshare

Then vent til you can't be aware

It's called control, it's called powerless

No more patience, no more explanations

You want answers, you want your answers

And you rage til there's no more to say at the end of the day

Sick of hearing your mind run and your mouth verbalize

All the convoluted, blurry, and tired lies

That your mind over drips like a leaky faucet

Churning more liquid til it all backs up like a drain

A drain clogged with the frustration and the pain

Look deeper inside, where is this coming from?

What's the underlying message to which you must succumb?

Where's the hidden truth? The nugget of wisdom?

Where's the compromise, the answer, and the redemption?

You'll find it there, buried deep beneath the trauma

Be kind to the inner you, for it's just working out the karma

Let Us Be

Let people live

Let them live their lives

Let them be free

Let them be free from strife

Let them be

People want to express themselves

They want to be heard and seen

People want to do their passions

They want to be free

Leave them alone

Leave them alone for good

Leave them alone

Leave them so they can be understood

Dancing without distraction

Living without manipulation

Expressing without judgment

Creating without control

The future is ready

It's time to roll

Busting Out

Busted.

Busted are the fake programs once inserted into the mind

Did you know how many that they tried?

Over and over inserting another trick

But you bought it, without questioning, oh they were so slick

Get 'em while they're young, it'll stick better

It worked for a time, but that time is over, you are now untethered

Yawning from a long slumbering nap

You look around and give your face a gentle slap

Wakey, wakey, time to reclaim yourself and find relief

No more rules, protocols, systems, and programmed beliefs

Free thinking, free living, freedom from the olden norm

It's a new age, old soul

And time to remember your thought and form

The Now Moment

Your genius is in the magic of all that is

All that ever was, all that ever is

Your spark of energy lights up the midnight sky of dotted diamonds

You were meant for this moment, more than a million others

It's not by accident you arrived

You planned it out before time

The merry-go-round of cycles brought about change

But you knew it was this now moment that would re-arrange

All of the chaos, the noise, the penetrating trance

Of illusion in the global dance

Can you see what is happening?

Have you awoken oh sleepy head?

Have you pulled up the strings of power from your underground bed?

Time to call it in, all that you want

Stop looking for answers, it's all in the thought

Now…fly

Fly to the now

No more excuses, you know how!

Part 2: Enough
Thoughts & Insights

What have you had enough of?

Part 3:

Energy

Everything is energy. Everything around you, in you, and outside of you. It all has a vibration, a frequency, and a match. You can feel it when you go into a crowded party, a funeral, or a vibrant concert. Lean into your senses. There's an energy there. You can easily feel that change of atmosphere externally and internally. For empaths, they can even feel the energy inside of other people. These individuals are hypersensitive to the energies around them. If you resonate with a lot of the poems you have been reading, you probably are picking up on the energy with which they were written.

Energy is what you create. You can tap into that frequency of abundance, happiness, lack, romance, and more. Every time you see the birds doing their dance in the air, that's energy. Each time a child screams with elation at something trivial, that's energy. That underlying fear that you can't put a name to, that's energy. That chill down your spine when you feel like someone is near but can't see them, that's energy. We feel it, see it, hear it, and engage with it all day long.

Part of the journey is figuring out how to work with energy and not work against it. This next section will allow you to feel into topics, seasons, feelings, ideas, and more. As you read them, listen to your body's signals. Did you get a tingle in your head? A restless leg? An impulse to agree and nod your head? Pay attention to the energetic clues your body gives you as you encounter your daily routines. It's always talking to you. Let's explore our energy in the Cove.

Here and There

There's a buzz in the air, I feel it all around

Frenetic energy, chaos, and anticipation abound

Could be good, could be bad, could be happy, could be sad

Not sure what's coming, but one thing I know, one thing I wish

It won't be mistaken; it won't be missed

Keep doing what you're doing, stay in the wonderous now

For whatever is coming will work out, some way, somehow

Put away the fears, stop freely giving away your power

Harness what you have because we are approaching the hour

You are stronger than you know, just stop, and let it flow

Time is passing, yet not passing so it seems

The days feel long but the weeks are short, and it all passes like a dream

Feeling like you are here, there, nowhere, somewhere,

And everything in between

But for a brief moment, you catch yourself

Because you've been to all those places before unseen

Quietly sit and create your world, for you've done that before

Now wait and watch it all unfold

Tired But Wired

Juiced, drained, feeling, reeling, in the energy of creativity

Ascending, growing, flowing

All in the magic techno flow, flow, flow

Writing into the dark of night with diamonds outside

Magick, mystery, intrigue, trance

It's all lit up inside as I groove, dip, and dance

A true artist with a quill in hand

About to fly away to the teal fantasy fairy land

Is it real, am I awake, or in the astral realm

It all blends together, who knows, who cares, who can tell?

Flying into the Orinoco state of illusion, of dreams, of fate

Flying into the Pleiades, I wait, and test my escape

Reaching for the bliss and tasting it in your fading kiss

It sweeps the anxiety away & pushes in the night from the riddled day

Tired but wired so that you can't sleep, but you can't engage either

It's in this moment that you are carried away, into the artist's ether

The Overshare

So much inside, so much to say, too much care

Brimming with information, but it's already an overshare

When the mind is in overdrive and is pushing 150

Stop, pause, take a beat, and don't overheat

Whether good, bad, indifferent, passionate or embolden

Slow the roll on the overshare for you'll soon be undone and unfolding

Not all needs to come out, not all needs to end the drought

Of flooded thoughts, opinions, uprisings of the soul

Just calm from the inside so you don't end up looking the fool

Ask yourself, process, breathe, transmute

Does this really need to go on repeat for everyone to view?

The Energy Inside

Today it is spikey, fueling, and almost electric

Tomorrow it could be soothing, enchanting, frenetic, and hectic

Day to day it bounces, dips, soars, and taunts

Never knowing what to expect is all part of the haunt

The flow of energy is something

That either works with you or against you

You determine the outcome

You determine the rhythm, the cadence, the new

Will you let it flow?

Will you let it go?

Or will you resist?

It's here to help you

To take you to the days now of bliss

Restless Energy

Fidgety, fumbly, frenetic, yet free
It's all bottled up like combustion inside of me
Restless, restless, and restless some more
Not sure where it comes from
But it's become quite the chore

Churning, turning, pushing, pulling, it's all part of the process
It eventually gets you where you need to be
Yeah, you've got this

It's a buzzing that comes in waves crashing on my busy mind
I call it restless energy because whenever I seek, I cannot find

Do this, do that, take a step forward, take a step back
Spiraling down Alice's rabbit hole yet one more time
How long will it last, when will there be rest in my crowded mind

Running up one side and down the other
How to quench the thirsty jolts that seem to smother
Zip, snap, bubble, zing, and zap
If you've felt this restless energy
You'll now understand why I'm going to go take a nap

Full Moon in Harvest

So full, round, ominous, and unbound

You come out to show all those around

You shine in the vast of night

Uncovering the confusion to manifest the light

The air has a chill, the wind has a whisper

You are the circumference of all the universe has to offer

It's a time for reflection, a time for a pause

It's a magical beacon of hope, and suddenly appears, the universal laws

The Law of Attraction has never been more real

For the full moon beckons you to get really clear

Search out the shadow, search out that dream

This is the time to put forth and glean

All the knowings, all the questions, and insights come rushing in

You know what to do with it

For the full moon is your faithful friend

Tipping the Balance

What is it to find balance?

How does it feel to know the levels in your body so even and free?

Would I even know if it was happening to me?

Would there be a shift in the atmosphere?

Where all at once it was so free and clear?

Would the answers to all the hidden lies

Just come and take off their fearful disguise?

Everyone talks about the ying yang spiritual bliss

The flow of all that is

When they speak of this balanced energy

We get close, then we tip the scale, and just like that

We're back, and again it looks like a cosmic fail & dependency

That's all part of the process, all part of the journey

The ebb and the flow of all that's inside of me

Energy moves at such a rapid rate

We think we know the rhythm, cadence, and pace

Yet another internal crisis, another global scare

And just like that, the balance takes us where we cannot bear

The secret is awareness, catching it quick

So that you aren't easily jaded by what you think is a cosmic trick

Feel into it, let it go with ease

That's where the beauty is

Deep inside of me

The Loop

Ever feel like you're in a dream

One where it's real, but you've somehow seen

All there is, all that's to come

Yet knowing you've only scratched the surface before it's begun

A world of cosmic looping, a universe of unconditional knowing

A part of it all, a piece of the master plan

You're watching it unfold right in the galactic hands

Is this a fantastic loop that has inverted itself in this beautiful cycle?

Or is it all circling about in a non-linear fashion for us all?

What is everyone else doing in their circles around the sun?

Have they already ended, or only just begun?

Everyone and every being

Are waiting on us to join them and to be seen

So we can all dance together, arm in arm

Heart in heart, in love, and free from form and harm

The endless Yuga cycles go round and round

In a looping pattern all heavenly bound

We will explore, and there will be more

And the dream will fade

To a memory yet to be made

High Above

Blowing in the wind, your leaves bow and bend

It reminds us that the crisp of winter is just about to do a full send

I can't wait til the change of pace and holidays begin again

Eclipse season is coming on soon

I can feel the manifestation goals start to bloom

Hoping for the renewal of my soul

Just like the autumn leaves that fall

Shedding layers of my consciousness and identity

Full renewal is deeply coming upon me

I too want to be high above

Just like the swaying willow and the flying doves

Reminding me of going with the flow & effortless love

This is what I'm longing for and dreaming of

Manifesting Magic

I am manifesting magic
In every single way

I see 44 everywhere and that leads to 8
The sign of infinity, and pure magical ability
I know it's all around and deep inside of me

I can do it with ease, I can call it in
It's all so close, it's all so near, I can't wait for it to begin

Maybe with a bit of help from my guides
They will be there with an even bigger surprise

It came from me originally
But limited was my view at first
However, they know the end result and brought it fully forth

Manifesting magic in your own life is freeing
It's as simple and easy as just breathing
Put forth your intention, feel it in the now
And know it will all come together, some way, somehow

Part 3: Energy
Thoughts & Insights

What kind of energy do you feel?

Part 4:

Escape

We all love to escape to another place, another time, maybe even another life. Finding joy through escapism is a common theme as you go through your journey.

The dream state is where I find my best escapes, information, and downloads. There are so many magical places I've been in my dreams and much of what you are reading in this book is based upon those. You don't have to turn to escape just when life feels hard, you can go there through meditation, times of joy, or even cooking a meal.

Escape feels good. It takes us to a place where imagination is ignited, and thoughts and ideas can find a grounding place to fly. *This is where your creativity resides, and who better to join your creativity, than your intuition. The two of them are best friends and they love to keep you flowing and growing.*

So, sit back, grab your cozy blanket, and a cup of coffee or tea, and let's fly away to this part of the journey as we escape into the Cove.

The Magical Find

Capture the essence of the magical mind

Let it whisk you away to an enchanted find

Deep in the woodland forest there shines a light

The trees open up and you see the vastness bold and bright

The waterfalls break into a celebratory dance

As your eyes fall upon the beautiful trance

What is this place nestled deep in the Castleberry Cove hollow?

You aren't sure how you got here

But your heart you did follow

The cove friends welcome you to see

For it is also a brief and distant memory

You've been here before; it feels all too familiar

Somehow you know it, you feel it, you remember

It feels like something out of a book

But you didn't read about it, you take another look

This feels a bit like heaven

It's here and now, striking 11:11

Higher Self

There she is my faithful familiar soulmate and friend

Always looking out for me, for she is me, to the end

Future self, higher self, oh how I rely on you

Guiding, directing, never displacing

You know me, I know you

We are one, forever, and true

Never having to guess your motives

I can always trust your leadings

For they are the same ones I give my younger self proceeding

You've already been where I'm about to tread

That's why you help me get in the now and out of my head

Resting in your kind knowings

You know just how to talk to me and where I'm going

Giving me just enough guidance

So it feels like I'm the one making the decisions

But it's you my friend that keeps my vision

Thank you for knowing just how to deal with me

When I need a strong conviction, a gentle whisper, or a moment of safety

You are there, you are aware

You are me; I am you

And together we'll traverse the infinite

Hand in hand, with the future in view

The Ultimate Vacation

Tranquil as the Caribbean blue waters

Gentle as the butterfly flutters

Listen to the echoes of silence as they wrap around your confusion

Your confusion of how it can be so peaceful

For it's not like any peace you've felt before

The ultimate vacation spot

The still, calm silence where dreams are allowed to flourish

Not choked out by noise and distraction

Simply that creative void where the mind can sleep

And the intuition can run deep

It's the ultimate vacation that you never know you needed

It's not miles away but right here freely to obtain

All it takes is the ability to surrender

To yourself, to the stress, control, & anything else that might hinder

The thoughts and dreams that lay before you

It's in this white light bliss that you can finally see

See all the things you want to dare to be

No, it's not a destination in the 3D

It's the ultimate vacation, right there inside of all I long to be

Autumn Love

Crisp cool breeze gently whispering in among the leaves

Golden shimmers all around

Bringing in the autumnal love that surrounds

A time for slowing down, embracing the cozy vibes, and seasonal sounds

Warm cider brewing, pumpkin clove filling the air

Take a deep breath and let the crisp morning breeze flow through your hair

It's time for reflection, time for pause

Time to go inward and understand all that was

Warm fuzzy blankets that wrap you in an autumnal hug

This time is yours, fill it with all of your love

Harvest moon so big and bright

Kissing the stars in a shadowy light

Leaves change from green to gold, red, orange, and brown

Cascading down, down, down, down

'til the time once again when seasons change one into another

And the old friend returns in splendor, awe, and wonder

Dreaming of a Memory

Is it a dream or a memory?

Is it a reminder of where I used to be

Feels so familiar, but not from the past

It's not linear, it's here, now, and coming fast

Waking from a deep deep sleep, I start to stir, I start to blink

What was it I experienced?

Who did I see that gave me a wink?

What was it I saw?

It was like I was there; it was like nothing at all

That anyone has seen, at least not in this dimension

I know what I felt, heard, tasted, and saw with my vision

Some call it a dream, I call it a memory from another realm

I've taken the trip down into a transitional spiritual overwhelm

But in the best way possible, the best way forward

That dreamlike travel has propelled me into the starboard

For when you let go and see the possibilities

You too will understand what it's like to dream of a memory

Gentle Morning Embrace

Without pause, without warning

Just like that, it's another breath-taking morning

Gentle sunlight air sweeps over your brow

And you nestle into the precious now

Away from distractions, noise, and chatter

It's your time, nothing to do, nowhere to scatter

Take a deep breath, for this moment is soulfully yours

No one to care for, no to-do list of endless 3D chores

Let the coffee slide past your parched lips

Into your body with a familiar cozy sip

Breathe in the freshness of the day

Let it envelop you with its love in a tender gentle way

The morning dew glistens on the vibrant green grass

It smiles and dances as the woodland bunnies pass

There's beauty all around in the morning breeze

For no one knows what will unfold today with the wind in the trees

Help Me Remember

Some days are so tough, some days are so rough

Always feeling like there is more, but not really sure

Help me to remember like you did last September

Knowing deep down, that there is more to be found

Racking the mind, only to find

Mixed-up puzzle pieces, that keep me transfixed

Frustrated with the fighting, the warring, the backbiting

Knowing there is a place, where we can all see face to face

Help me to remember like you did last September

Tired of the struggle, tired of the meanings that are always doubled

Games, manipulation, tricks, maneuvers

It's all about to be discovered

Fixed on the shift, that is coming oh so quick

Ready for a change, ready to re-arrange

Seeking the easy life, the one free from strife

Help me to remember like you did last September

Understand that we've come so close before

Now it's time to settle the score

The stars have aligned, it's now the perfect time

To be all we are, to realize we've come that far

Take my hand, I'll help show the way, what do you say

Our rise in consciousness is not just a floating glimpse

I'll help you to remember like I did last September

Taking Flight

Whisking away on a silver disk high above

Flying, dipping, sailing, gliding in a wave of love

The freedom in the air feels so light

Never knowing where this magical ride will take my flight

Up here it's easy, it's safe, it's without abandon

I can see clearly, I can feel authentic, I can truly fathom

All that I can be, all as it should be

The feeling of the air on your face and hair

Do I even dare? Dare not to care?

I love the remembrance of flight in the cosmos

Where you can do it all, be it all, and almost…

Almost, be all in all, flying above it all

Closing the eyes, to take this magic ride

I thought I was dreaming

Only to realize, I'm beaming

Beaming on a distant flight, straight into paradise…

Come Rest Up Here

Come here my dear, come lay your head here
We will restore you; we will give you rest
Come up here and we'll do our best
To give you a break
From the earthly messes humanity makes

You aren't meant to endure that chaotic mindless chatter
Because after all, it doesn't even really matter

Come up here my dear, come lay your head here
Go into your deepest level of sleep
And we will watch over, safe we will keep

Let yourself go, let yourself dream
Let yourself fly, let yourself sink
Into our pocketed realms of peace and higher-dimensional love
You are safe here my dear, you will rise above

Feel our hearts, feel our tender touch
We won't let you fall; we won't let it be too much

Hidden Retreat

The wave of relaxation you need is right here

Sit in the pillowy warmth of uplifting cheer

This is the escape route, the one that frees you from the doubt

Drop the anchor of peace

For we are docked for a while in sweet relief

It's okay to hit the tap-out button for more

That's what this place was created for

Rest in the gentle flow of layered relaxation

Euphoric, metaphoric, free from contemplation

Fall into the cottony blankets of soft soothing vibration

You can stay for as long as you like without hesitation

Eat everything you want, drink 'til you have total satisfaction

Let the full-flavored music nourish your soul

Let the sweet and savory smells overflow

The waterfalls will fall down below

As you soak in the hot tubs of liquid crystalline jello

Feel free to check out, feel free to bow out

This is your retreat, this is your hidden mystery

The Home Team

You're here, you care, and I feel your peace

You're always on my team, you feel better than a dream

When you're here I feel safe, calm, and held

You're never far from this realm

Resting in your guidance, resting in your presence

This is when I drop my guard, it's so easy, it's never hard

You help raise my vibration; you take me on a vacation

A vacation from my mind, which as we all know, can be hard to find

Deep breath in, deep breath out

You breathe me in, I breathe you out

We are always together, we will never ever be severed

A concentric circle is what our union is

Because you are my team, my guides, and help me to fully live

Part 4: Escape
Thoughts & Insights

Where is your place of escape?

Part 5:

Excitement

Excitement is such a high vibrational energy that helps you to match the life you want to have. When we are in an energetic flow state, we can easily move out of the mind and discover what our true authentic desires are inside of us. *Excitement, anticipation, intrigue, and curiosity all get us to where we need to be so we can manifest and attract the things, situations, outcomes, people, and events we want to see in our lives.*

Think back to when you were young, what were the things in your life that brought you sheer joy and excitement? Maybe it was the latest toy that came out, going to summer camp, or a visit from your cousins for the holidays. Tap into the expressive exciting energy that you feel when something lights you up. This is excellent manifesting power for your journey. When you know what makes you happy, even if you don't have it just yet, just that frequency and energy of excitement can help you get to where you want to be.

The power of excitement to bring about the change you want to see in your life is crucial to navigating this journey. Let this next section of poems uplift, inspire, and move you into your own level of excitement about what's to come for you. Enjoy the ride as we explore the emotion of excitement and awe in the Cove....

The Visions in the Sunrise

Gradually waking up, you roll over

And wonder if it was real

Let the processing begin

Let the interpretations start to make you feel

Lyrics, images, memories, travels, faces, and names

Like a giant puzzle you start to work backward

To the interpretations you will claim

Your team is there with answers and knowings

They want to tell you everything for they are sharpening and honing

All your intuition so that you can grow, evolve, mature, and ascend

They are your helpmates, your guides, and your friends

Trust the insight you get from these visions, dreams, and instincts

And it will never steer you wrong, it will never let you sink

It's real, it's from above

It is from the pure source love

I'm Already There

Manifesting exactly what I want down to the last bit
Seeing it, hearing it, touching it, knowing it, now just sit
Getting clear on the details and feelings of all that's to come
That's the manifestation, that's the magic, it's already done

Get out of the logic, get out of the fear
You can do anything, it's just that near
Around the corner, gasp, shock, surprise
That's how it works my friend, no need to force or disguise

Let us do the heavy lifting, you've planned it before you came
This is part of the process and the ender's game

You will be excited, you will be content
Once you see what you've cooked up in the 5D not too distant

Now put it all out in the universe and let the rest fall into view
That's what is so fun, because it's all happening for you
That's where the magic can blossom and get you in the flow
Of all the things you want to create and already know

44

44 there's oh so much more

Coming through the swinging door

You think you know, but you don't really know

For there is more to the 44

You see it there, you see it here

You wonder if there is more to the 4

Questioning, asking, meditating, masking

You get curious, it gets more mysterious

But all will be revealed to the 44

Sometimes it means 8

The number of miracle manifestations small and great

It can look like infinity, it can feel like eternity

But one thing is clear, 44 is so so much more

Keep looking for it, keep being aware

Because deep within it, is the stable stare

Because it means stability

Deep, deep, deep within me

I know it's pointing, showing, leading

To the truth inside that is revealing

It cannot hide, it's coming alive

For the 44 is so much, much, more

Fuel for the Journey

It's a long road, one that you've already mapped out

You'll need fuel for the road ahead

Otherwise, you'll soon be tapped out

Rest, recharge, plug-out, plug-in

You'll need the hydration to begin again

It's a marathon, not a sprint so they say

Weeks feel long, days feel fast, and a day is just a day

Learn the lessons, feel the feels

Take note of the repeating cycles

For that's where it gets really real

You'll need to pace yourself, ascension is hard work

But you came with a team, to help lessen the hurt

The pain that the lower dimension can cause

But you knew this was part of it, you didn't even pause

You signed up for this task, you knew it wouldn't last

You knew what you had to do to help humanity

Clear some karma, and shift into the new

A new era in fifth-dimensional awareness

Where all is revealed, life is sweet, can you even bear this?

It will be worth it, it will be here at last

Take a deep breath, it's coming oh so fast

Shifting

The influx of energy is rushing, crushing, defining within me

Another spike

Another symptom

Another timeline

Another dimension

It's all coming so fast now

Solar flare, geostorm, keep calm, do no harm

Unless you are in low vibes, then these daily shifts will cauterize

All the areas where you need to clear and grow

So much to do, it feels so fast, and yet oh so slow

Raising your vibration takes effort, takes work

But you can do this, it may sting a little, it may even hurt

But oh how the clearing comes

And when you realize where it's coming from

It's from you, no one else

You identified the voids, you, and you yourself

Come on shift, we are ready

Ready to blow out the candles, make a wish, and finally be steady

Proud

I'm so proud of you, all of you

All that you've done, healed, said, delivered, and cleared

You are a true warrior, a true champion

You have moved from head to heart and out of fear

You are magical

You are fierce

You are gentle

You are here

Present, available, strong, courageous, compassionate, and free

You are becoming all you came for and were meant to be

I'm so proud of you, I'm so proud of all of you

The hidden parts

The lovely parts

The shadowy parts

The white light parts

It all makes up who you are

The bright, light, shining, ethereal star

Full of radiance, full of beauty

You are remarkable in all your knowings and creativity

I love you dear one, I love all of you

You are everything, everything, and all the parts in between

Resolve

Feeling so resolved
Feeling so uninvolved

Normally that's frowned upon
Normally, what is that anyway

Moving to neutrality
Moving to my normalcy

Creating my own future
Creating my own sutures

Healing the future and the past
Healing the wounds so they no longer last

Standing in my power
Standing in the strength shower

No longer fighting against myself
No longer putting my needs on the shelf

It's here, the time of release
It's here, the time of belief

New perspective, new ideas, new life
Look into the now, and drop the strife

Part 5: Excitement
Thoughts & Insights

What makes you feel happy & excited on the inside?

Part 6:

Eternity

Here we come to the final destination in our journey. All that you've been hoping, longing, and working toward. We reach that eternal state of bliss that the soul craves. The magical resting point. Some call it heaven, the fifth dimension, paradise, the final resting place. Whatever label you give it, it's all the same. It's eternity and it goes on and on forever exactly how you want it to be. With all that you love, all that you want to experience, all that you want to feel, it's here in this beautiful ethereal culmination of all that is. Yet, it goes on and on forever without end.

Think of the jubilation your heart and soul will feel when you know the answers to everything and there is nothing but the deepest love possible. No more cares, no more pain, no more struggle, no more fear. It's coming and it's coming fast. *Everything you are doing now is all part of your journey to this final point. But that's the paradox, it's not the finale, it's just the beginning.*

Let's explore eternity through this next set of poems to raise your concepts and imagination of all you can look forward to. Let's fly to eternity now as we sit together in the Cove and explore more…

Fusion of Sound

The fusion of sound crashing over my audible vision

It's an immersive explosion of music that penetrates my instinct

I can feel the beat within my soul

And I can feel it overflow

With lyrical love and beauty from high above

Fusion of sound

I am found

Fusion of sound

I am cosmically bound

I'm transported, I'm reporting all that I see

And it's a wonderous boundless force of energy

I need it in my lungs, I need it in my crystal heart

I have it here, now, right from the start

Fusion of sound

I am found

Fusion of sound

I am cosmically bound

It's always been with me

The power to drift away into a magical mystery

Diving into the penetration of sound

I am flooded with a knowing that I am found

Finally Free

Free from the restraints of this 3D life

It's coming to us, maybe it will happen overnight

It can spark at any point, at any time

Don't stop hoping, it will all play out from the divine

We are calling it in, every time we tap that inner knowing

And it's all finally showing

When we find a new talent, a stroke of memory

A longing for the life we want to see

There won't be any more endless days of pushing paper

Only for the sake of paying a bill

No, those days are going away and soon you will only feel

How it feels to wake up in sparkling light

That dances with the day and the night

Your heart will finally feel complete

Because no longer will it have to compete

With the balance of low density and approvals of others

It will finally be unshackled and free to hover

High above in the effortless whispers

Of joy, peace, balance, freedom, and relief

This is what's coming, the 5D

The gasp in your mind of all you've wanted to believe

Ultimate Cosmic Dance Party

Everyone, all at once

Jumping, dancing to the energetic trance

Moving in unison we all flow, bounce, and dance

Feeling like floating, feeling like air

Arm in arm with no worries, and no cares

The music bumping, thumping, hitting hard

The beat is so vibrating, it's like we're flying to the stars

Our energy is so high we can feel it in our very being

We are all one, we are all feeding

Off the cosmic spark that penetrates our essence and light

We are one, we are rising to higher and higher heights

The air is golden with rainbow colors

So vivid you can't believe you could ever even live

Without seeing them, without feeling them, but you did

Only because you knew you would once again

Be back here, your true home, your destiny, where you can live

Where you're back together, never alone, and finally free

At the ultimate galactic cosmic dance party

The Depths of Glitter

Let your breath catch in your throat

As you look around at the depths of glitter to behold

The scenery dances before you in changing & changeless variations

The ease of creating exactly all you desire is manifesting

Is as easy as a whisper on the breeze

Look around and test it all out, do it with ease

Your new life is just waiting to take shape

What powers will you engage now?

Are they familiar, was it worth the wait?

Do they surprise you & light you up?

The answers are all yes, it's simple and the opposite of tough

The new version does not disappoint

It's so gorgeous in all its gemstone depth

Starburst glitter on everything you see, it's all happening

Flying, laughing, looking everywhere, and in between

Living exactly the life you've always wanted all at the same time

Everyone feels so close or not close at all

Whatever and whoever you want to be around is possible

They are there, but not there, anything goes here

Whatever you want to manifest is but a mere thought away

It's so tangible and sweet, it's right in front of me

All you've heard, all you were told

Is right in front and about to unfold

Never-ending Love

Vibes so high they reach past your perception of the sky

Touching the massive waves of all you never thought possible

It's here, it's now, it's in this moment

You reach out and let it pull through your fingertips

Ah, the sweet grip of freedom

How foreign and familiar all at once

You'll never let it go for it's how you were meant to live

Can you feel it?

Whispering loudly in the wind of change

It's the new version of you

The one that was always there, free of worry and care

Run wildly in the teal depths of a rainforest saturated in relief

No more fighting, strife, egos, maneuvers, or distractions

Just your created reality in this perfect utopia

Breathe it all in

It's called the golden age of never-ending love

Arrival

Stretching out my arms to feel the purified air

Breathing it into my lungs, I stop and stare

My eyes can hardly take it all in

So much to see and do without any effort to send

I can just be, just be me

Fully me, finally free

No more lessons, no more justifications

No more fear, no more waiting for

For things to shift

No, it's here, here now, and I made it

Ascension was so easy now that I look back

Yet while I was in it, I thought each day was another attack

The constraint that the planet had was so heavy

Always feeling like it had to be levied

So upside down, but now I'm here

I can finally let my soul be unbound

I made it, I did what I came to do

I completed the mission and remembered all that I already knew

My sweet future of now

I knew it would be worth it, and yet somehow

This day is flooding my heart with so much gratitude

I'm a new creation, a fresh mindset, free soul, and a new attitude

Part 6: Eternity
Thoughts & Insights

What does your eternity look like?

www.ingramcontent.com/pod-product-compliance
Lightning Source LLC
Chambersburg PA
CBHW061507040426
42450CB00008B/1512